EXCHANGE & MART
GUIDE TO

MOVING HOME

D1742947

GUIDE TO

MOVING HOME

Val Redding

JAVELIN BOOKS
POOLE · NEW YORK · SYDNEY

First published in the UK 1986 by Javelin Books,
Link House, West Street, Poole, Dorset BH15 1LL

Copyright © 1986 Javelin Books

Distributed in the United States by
Sterling Publishing Co., Inc.,
2 Park Avenue, New York, NY 10016

Distributed in Australia by
Capricorn Link (Australia) Pty Ltd,
PO Box 665, Lane Cove, NSW 2066

British Library Cataloguing in Publication Data

Redding, Valerie
 Exchange & Mart guide to moving home.
 1. House buying—England   2. House selling—England.
 I. Title
 333.33'8'0942   HD1379

ISBN 0 7137 1895 1

Photography by the David Bampton Studio, Southampton.

Typeset by Poole Typesetting (Wessex) Ltd
Printed in Great Britain by Cox & Wyman, Reading, Berks.

Contents

Introduction

There is something very special about owning your own home, but the business of buying and selling property is a complex one which requires very careful preparation and organisation if disasters are to be avoided. Whether you are a first-time buyer or experienced home owner, it is also very important that you should understand exactly what you are doing, and why it has to be done. Mistakes are costly — you can't afford to make any at all!

If you are buying, or selling, or doing both, this book will take you through the whole process step by step, explaining exactly what to do and how and when to do it. Part One deals with buying a property and Part Two with selling a property, and throughout the book you will find a series of checklists to use in conjunction with the information supplied. The Appendix gives some advice on buying a house in Scotland, where the law concerning property is somewhat different from that in England and Wales.

PART ONE:
BUYING A HOME

1 · What Can You Afford?

Before looking for a property to buy, it is important to know exactly how much money you can afford to pay for it. Of course you may be lucky enough to have adequate cash readily available to buy your house outright, but for most of us the money must be raised by way of a mortgage, and we must begin our venture into the world of property by finding out exactly how much mortgage we are able to obtain and how much we can afford to pay for our new house.

Far too many people make the mistake of guessing how much they can afford and enter into negotiations only to find they are unable to raise enough money to complete their transaction. This is probably the most common cause of 'chains' of sales falling through. There are in fact several key questions which must be answered if you are not to be drawn into such a situation. So let us begin by finding out what these questions are, and then discussing where to go for the answers.

WHAT TYPE OF MORTGAGE IS MOST SUITABLE FOR YOU?

The Straight Repayment (or Annuity) Mortgage
Here you borrow a lump sum over a period of years and the

interest plus part of the capital is repaid per month. At the beginning of the term the amount of interest repaid per month is very high, but decreases as the term progresses. If interest rates should go up, you can arrange to extend the term of the loan to cover the extra costs without increasing your monthly repayments, but because this could extend the term for an indefinite period it is better to increase the monthly repayments if you can possibly afford to. This type of mortgage should be accompanied by a Mortgage Protection Insurance Policy, which is a type of life insurance to cover the outstanding amount of the debt should the borrower die before the loan has been paid off in full.

The Endowment Mortgage (life assurance linked)

Here you borrow a lump sum over a period of years and this lump sum is left outstanding for the full term of the advance. The loan is linked to an Endowment Life Assurance Policy (preferably a 'with profits' policy) and each month you repay the premium together with the interest on the loan. At the end of the term the policy matures to pay off the loan in full, and, where a 'with profits' policy has been taken out, any extra bonuses are paid to you in a lump sum. If you should die before that time the loan is paid off in full by the policy. If interest rates rise during the term of this mortgage, the borrower must increase his monthly repayments to cover the rise in order that the term of the advance continues to run concurrently with the policy. It is possible to transfer the policy to another property if you want to move again later. It should be noted that most lenders charge a higher rate of interest for an endowment mortgage, usually in the region of $\frac{1}{2}$ per cent.

The Low Start Mortgage
(of special interest to first-time buyers)

Most building societies and other lenders appreciate the

special difficulties first-time buyers face when it comes to raising a mortgage, and there are several schemes in operation which first-time buyers might consider, the most popular being the low start mortgage. As the name indicates, the repayments at the beginning of the term are lower and gradually increase as the term progresses. This type of advance is most suitable if the borrower's income is likely to increase and his status improve as the term of the loan continues. First-time buyers should make a special effort to find out from various lenders what savings and mortgage schemes they offer, and decide for themselves which scheme is most suited to their particular circumstances.

HOW MUCH CAN YOU BORROW?

Most lenders rely on a 'multiple' system to assess how much money they can lend you. These multiples vary considerably. For instance, one lender may allow $2\frac{1}{2}$ times your annual salary plus one time any secondary income (e.g. wife's salary) whilst another may add both annual salaries together and multiply the whole by two. Overtime, bonuses, commission etc will only be considered if they are received on a regular basis. If interest rates are high the multiple will probably be low, but if interest rates are low and funds more freely available the multiples will possibly be higher.

The lender will require the following basic information in order to calculate figures for you:

a) Your basic salary (gross).

b) Overtime, bonuses, commission etc, if these are received on a regular basis.

c) Details of any secondary salary to be included.

d) Any other income available.

e) Details of any heavy financial commitments you may already have.

Restrictions apply to the type of property on which building societies will advance money. A high-percentage mortgage on thatched properties may be difficult to obtain.

f) How much of your own money will be contributed towards the total.
g) If you are self-employed, up-to-date accounts for the previous few years.

Most lenders will advance only 75–80 per cent of the full purchase price of the property, or the Society's valuation of that property (whichever is the lower). If a higher advance is made, some kind of additional security will be required, such as a Mortgage Indemnity Policy or Guarantee Bond. The borrower will have to pay a one-off premium for this cover. If you think you may need one, check how the premium is to be paid, i.e. whether added to the loan, or as a separate extra charge.

The lender may also impose various restrictions on the advance. For instance, he may not be prepared to consider a high advance on the following:

a) A flat above a certain level.

b) A property built before a certain year.

c) A property with a sitting tenant.

d) A leasehold property with only a few years of the lease left to run.

e) A property which does not meet the standard of construction required.

Each lender will have his own rules and regulations, so find out what they are before you start looking for a property, in case it should not be suitable for the mortgage you require.

HOW MANY YEARS WILL IT TAKE TO PAY OFF THE LOAN?

This will depend a great deal on your present age. The cost of repayments will obviously be higher if you repay over a shorter period. The usual period is 25 years. Some lenders will increase that period, but most expect the mortgage to be repaid in full by the time you retire.

WHAT IS A TOP-UP LOAN?

If the main source of your loan is not adequate it may be possible to arrange a further top-up advance to make up any shortage. This is usually arranged via a bank or insurance company and interest rates are very high indeed.

Some 'package deals', where 100 per cent advances are offered, are made up with top-up loans where the main advance is not enough. Unfortunately this is not always made clear to the inexperienced applicant, so if you require a high advance in relation to your income, from whatever source, especially if you are a first-time buyer, make sure you know exactly where the funds are coming from and what the repayments are going to be. If you are in any doubt, consult an independent solicitor or accountant for advice. A half-hour informal chat will cost very little but could save you a lot of money and a great deal of worry later on.

Under no circumstances take on any commitment you may not be able to afford to repay or that will restrict you in any way from re-selling at a later date.

WHAT INTEREST RATES WILL BE CHARGED ON THE LOAN?

Interest rates vary considerably and there are often 'threshold' loans above which higher interest rates are charged. For instance, one lender may charge an extra $\frac{1}{2}$ per cent on loans above £20,000 and a further $\frac{1}{2}$ per cent on loans above £25,000, whilst another may not charge extra until the figure of £30,000 is reached. Check which rate will be applicable in your case and make a note for comparisons later.

HOW MUCH WILL THE LOAN COST TO REPAY?

You will need to know: a) the cost per month; b) the cost per £1,000 borrowed per month. This second figure will be most useful if you need to do some last-minute adjustments, perhaps because you have been drawn into negotiations where the last few hundred pounds could make all the difference.

WHAT TAX RELIEF WILL YOU GET?

Tax relief is available on the interest paid on advances up to £30,000 (1986 figure). There is no relief on any amount above this figure. There is no relief on Life Assurance Policies (including Endowment Policies) taken out after 13 March 1984.

You may need to shop around for a high mortgage on high-rise flats.

With MIRAS (Mortgage Interest Relief At Source) you pay the lender your monthly repayment *less* the relevant tax relief and the lender claims the tax from the Inland Revenue, although some banks will expect full payment per month and reimburse your current account with the relevant amount of tax. Lenders will give you quotations for monthly repayments before and after tax has been deducted.

WHAT ABOUT VALUATION FEES
(sometimes known as Inspection Fees)?

At the time of applying for your mortgage, you will be required to pay a valuation or inspection fee. This fee is used by the lender to instruct a surveyor to report on the condition and value of the property to be mortgaged. The lender needs to know what security the property offers to support the loan you require, and it is on this assessment of value that the final offer of an advance will be made. Charges are scaled in relation to the price of the property to be mortgaged and according to the *depth* of the survey to be carried out. There is usually a choice. You should be sent a copy of the report, but it must be remembered that this will not be a full structural survey. If you feel you need one, however, the fee will be slightly lower if you instruct the same surveyor as the lender so that he can carry out both jobs at once. The lender will give you further details on request.

If you would like an independent report, the Royal Institute of Chartered Surveyors offer a very competitive 'Home Buyers Report and Valuation' obtainable from any chartered surveyor and offered at a realistic price — well worth considering if you have any worries about the value and condition of the property to be purchased, but do not want the extra expense of a full structural survey.

An eighteenth century character property reputed to be haunted – a comprehensive survey would be essential if it were to be sold today.

WHAT INSURANCES WILL YOU NEED?

We have already mentioned Mortgage Protection Policies and Endowment Life Assurance Policies.

An insurance to cover fire and other risks to the building is always a condition of granting a mortgage. The lender will arrange this and advise you of the premiums based on the cost of re-building the property should it be totally destroyed by, say, flood or fire. This cover should be increased as the value of the property increases (most lenders insist on this anyway) and is payable once per annum. The lender often pays the first premium with effect from the day that contracts are exchanged, when, for insurance purposes, the property becomes the buyer's responsibility. This initial premium will be accounted for when your mortgage money finally comes through. If it is not done in this way, then be prepared to pay the required premium at the time of exchange of contracts. Ask the lender, or check with your solicitor well in advance, so that you know what will be happening.

It is wise to take out an insurance to cover the contents of the house for fire and theft. Premiums are based on the value of the contents, so make a list for ease of reference and make sure the policy is dated from the day you move in. Don't leave it until later — you could be burgled on the very first night!

It should be noted that although the lender will arrange for these policies to take effect, and will obtain quotations for you (except fire and theft), you are quite at liberty to approach an insurance company of your own choice, although it must be approved by the lender. Any reputable insurance company will give you quotations and, here again, there is no harm in shopping around for comparisons!

WHAT ABOUT ANY EXISTING MORTGAGE YOU MAY HAVE?

If you have a house to sell then you probably have an existing mortgage which must be redeemed (paid off) when you move. Arm yourself with any reference numbers you may have relating to your present loan and contact your lender to find out what this redemption figure will be. You may have to pay a 'redemption charge' which is usually three months' extra interest, but in some cases this can be waived if you receive another advance from the same company.

Don't be put off by all these technicalities! Getting a mortgage isn't at all as complicated as it may seem. To refresh your memory, Checklist 1 sets out all the questions you need to ask and all the information you will need to give in order that the lender can work out figures and give you the necessary quotations. Rules and regulations, fees, 'multiples', and so on, vary from lender to lender, so it is to your advantage to shop around for the information you need and make notes for comparisons later on.

Now you know what questions to ask, let us consider where to go to get your answers.

1) What type of mortgage is most suitable for you?
   a) Straight repayment mortgage.
   b) Endowment mortgage (with profits or non-profit?).
   c) Low start mortgage.
   d) Any other scheme the lender may suggest that could be suitable.
2) How much can you borrow?
3) What multiples will be used?
4) Will you need a mortgage indemnity policy or guarantee bond? If so:
   a) How much will it cost?
   b) Will the cost be added to the loan or due as a separate payment?
5) What restrictions — if any — could be imposed on the loan?
6) How many years will it take to repay the loan?
7) Will you need a top-up loan? If so:
   a) How much will it cost?
   b) Could it restrict you from re-selling profitably later on?
8) What interest rate will be charged?
9) How much will the repayments be?
   a) Per month.
   b) Per £1,000 borrowed per month.
10) What tax relief will you get?
11) What will the valuation fee be?
12) What insurances will you need and what are they likely to cost?
13) If you already have a mortgage which will have to be redeemed:

a) What outstanding amount will become payable?

b) What redemption charges will there be?

14) Any other questions you may wish to ask the lender.

The Information you need to give

1) Your basic salary (gross).
2) Overtime, bonuses, commission etc (if received on a regular basis).
3) Details of any secondary income to be included.
4) Any other income available.
5) Details of any heavy financial commitment you may already have, e.g. maintenance repayments if you are divorced, H.P., any others.
6) How much of your own money you will be contributing.
7) If you are self-employed, you will need current up-to-date accounts.
8) Details of your present employment.

BUILDING SOCIETIES

These will probably be your first choice, and if you are already an investor, or already have a mortgage with a building society, try that one first. Most building societies give preferential treatment to their investors, especially those who save a regular amount. If funds are limited first-time buyers and people moving on business will receive preferential treatment too, but don't be discouraged if you are not an investor. Many building societies will consider your case on its merits, so call in and ask!

19

BANKS

Here again, contact your own bank manager first. Banks, like building societies, use certain multiple rules to assess their loans. They also offer repayment and endowment mortgages and can advise on the appropriate insurance cover. But do make sure you know what interest rate is being charged as it may not be in line with the bank's basic rate, nor with the current building society rates of interest.

BROKERS

Mortgage brokers do not lend money themselves, though they know where sources are currently available, especially at times when funds are limited. Often they can obtain advances for those 'difficult' cases which do not fit into the normal pattern of things. If a broker arranges a straight repayment

Building societies and banks compete for business in a busy high street. Shop around for the best possible deal.

mortgage for you he could charge you a fee of 2 per cent. If an endowment mortgage is arranged, however, he receives his commission from the insurance company based on the premiums you will be paying. It is as well to remember that, if you accept an endowment mortgage via a broker and subsequently cancel the policy within the first few years, he could claim any outstanding commission from you. However, he can only do this if the arrangement is made perfectly clear to you right from the beginning. Be very wary of any Broker who asks for a non-returnable deposit of any kind. If a deposit is lodged and he does not arrange a mortgage for you, or you do not take it up within six months, you are entitled to have it returned, less £1 administrative charges.

If you have any doubts at all *get everything in writing* and keep it somewhere safe in case you should need it later on. Since 1st December 1981 all *brokers* must register with the Insurance Brokers Registration Council, but anyone can call himself an 'agent', a 'consultant' or anything else. It is worth checking that the broker you approach is a member of the Council, so that you can be sure he will abide by their strict code of conduct. If you need to write a cheque for a valuation fee, make it payable to the lender and not the broker.

ON-SITE SALESMEN

If you are buying a new house, most sales representatives can arrange mortgages. Very often a lender may allocate a lump sum for the whole development on which the salesman can draw, or they may have special arrangements to advance mortgages to applicants who may not be investors with them. In any event, it will still be subject to your income; and, as we mentioned earlier, if that amount seems very high in relation to your salary, check where the extra funds are coming from.

Most estate agents can arrange mortgages. This agency has a busy building society section offering its customers every facility (courtesy Robert Silk & Partners).

In all cases, make sure you know the source of the loan, interest rates and full details. You may be able to do better by arranging your own finance.

ESTATE AGENTS

As part of their professional service, most estate agents are able to arrange mortgages for you via building societies, banks and other lenders, on the condition that you buy a property from their register. Most are direct agents for one or the other of these and as such can often push forward an application on your behalf at times when it would not be considered if you were to approach the lender direct.

COUNCIL HOUSE AND HOUSING ASSOCIATION TENANTS

The Housing Act 1980 and the Housing and Building Control Act 1984 gives council tenants, new town tenants and some tenants of housing associations the right to buy their homes, and recent legislation has increased the discount allowed to 42 per cent after two years of occupancy up to a maximum of 70 per cent. Full details can be obtained from your local authority, and are contained in the brochure *Your Right to Buy Your Home, A Guide for Council Tenants, New Town and Housing Association Tenants.*

You can obtain explanatory leaflets and brochures from all these sources, including repayment charts showing monthly amounts repayable in relation to the amount of the advance, current interest rates and the term of the advance. They also provide tables of survey fees and the type of survey covered. You can just walk in and ask, or better still make an appointment for an interview so that you have plenty of time to discuss everything in detail. Don't be too disappointed if

Council house tenants have the right to buy their homes. This house, now privately owned, is a credit to its present owner.

Many of the properties on this Council Development are now privately owned, providing quality homes in a pleasant environment.

the first person you approach is not able to offer you a mortgage right away. Always shop around, compare interest rates and the various mortgage schemes available, and assess which is most suitable for your particular requirements. Take into account any changes that might affect your status later on. For instance if you are relying on your wife's income to increase the loan and subsidise repayments, what would happen if she had to leave work for some reason? Could you manage if your overtime or commission was no longer forthcoming? Only *you* can judge accurately what you can afford and what you cannot!

It should be remembered that at this point you are only *making enquiries*. Although at least one lender will no doubt be prepared to consider a mortgage application from you under the terms and conditions you have discussed (agreed a mortgage in principle), don't be led into believing this is a definite mortgage offer — it is not. Such an offer will only be forthcoming once you have chosen a house to buy, submitted a formal mortgage application, a valuation has been carried out and references taken up. All this must be done to the satisfaction of the lender *before* a definite mortgage offer can be issued to you.

However, by now you will have a good idea of how much

money you can borrow, what the repayments are likely to be and whether an advance is readily available or not. You will also be in a position to decide which type of mortgage is most suitable. You will know what insurance cover is necessary, the cost of the relevant premiums and what sum you should set aside to cover valuation and survey fees. Most important of all, you will know where to go for your mortgage when the time finally comes. Later on you will find the information and deeper understanding you have gained absolutely essential if you are not to be drawn into an abortive transaction.

But it is still not enough to calculate exactly how much you can afford. So let us now see what other expenses are going to be incurred.

LEGAL FEES

Charges for conveyancing are now very competitive. Solicitors will quote you their fees on application, or you can use the services of an independent conveyancing company who specialise entirely in conveyancing and are not likely to be in court on another matter when you most need to speak to them. Reputable conveyancing companies are usually members of the National Association of Conveyancers, 2/4 Chichester Rents, Chancery Lane, London WC2A 1EJ, or the National Institute of Conveyancing Agents, 10 Upper Belmont Road, Bristol BS7 9BQ. To belong to these organisations the conveyancing company must have several years of practical conveyancing experience and have lodged an indemnity insurance for their client's accounts. There is usually a set fee for the conveyance, plus the following charges.

Stamp Duty (a tax on legal documents)

Currently (1986) stamp duty is 1 per cent of the total purchase price of the property, if that price is over £30,000.

Shared driveways and communal parking present problems. Make sure there are adequate facilities if you have two cars.

Local Searches

It is very important to know, before you commit yourself to buy a property, what environmental changes there are going to be which may affect the house once you move in. Your solicitor will therefore send a standard form to the local authority setting out questions relating to such matters as compulsory purchase orders, road improvements, new developments and so on. He will also make 'preliminary enquiries' from the vendor's solicitor concerning the property itself: i.e. boundaries, rights of way, shared access, extensions carried out by the present owner etc. In this way he is able to find out as much as possible about the property before exchange of contracts.

Land Registry Fee

The land register records the true ownership of each registered property (title), together with other details about the property. In some areas compulsory registration has been under way for some time, whilst in other areas the system is still in its infancy. When a change of ownership takes place, full details must be registered. Your solicitor will need to inspect the register in order to investigate the title, and ensure that the person selling to you is fully entitled to do so! If the title is unregistered his task is more difficult, as he will have to investigate the title deeds covering the previous 15 years or more. Fees for first registration are based on the purchase price of the property, but are slightly lower for transferring to a new owner.

Building Society Solicitor's Fee

You will also have to pay the fee for the solicitor acting on behalf of your lender. If your own solicitor acts in this capacity the fees will be reduced.

VAT

Value added tax must be allowed for.

Disbursements

Postage, telephone calls etc come under the heading of disbursements.

Some selling agents may offer 'package deals' which include the service of a solicitor, and some may offer to subsidise your legal costs through the solicitor of your choice. If you are introduced to a solicitor or conveyancing company via the selling agent, bear in mind that what you must have is *completely impartial* guidance and advice. Ask yourself if a solicitor affiliated to the selling agent would divide his loyalties between yourself and that agent. If you think not, then you may find such a package deal well worth consideration, but if you have any doubts at all, choose a solicitor or conveyancing company that is completely independent and has no connection whatsoever with the

27

selling agent or the vendor. One solicitor can deal with your sale and your purchase, but the same solicitor cannot act for both the vendor and the purchaser. Here the divided loyalties that would ensue are quite obvious. If you are not already in touch with a solicitor or conveyancing company, try your *Yellow Pages*. Telephone several companies and compare rates before you decide which one to instruct. When you have made up your mind, ring them back or write them a note to say you would like them to act on your behalf, and ask the name of the person to whom correspondence should be addressed. You will need this information later on.

You are perfectly entitled to undertake your own legal work, which will be less expensive, although it is not as easy as it may first appear and certainly not recommended unless you have some experience in this field or a good friend with the necessary expertise to help out! There are several books currently available which will be helpful if you are brave enough to tackle it yourself, including *The Legal Side of Buying a House* (Consumer's Association), *The Conveyancing Fraud* (Michael Joseph).

SELLING COSTS

If you sell your house yourself (privately) then you will certainly save money, but don't forget to allow for advertising costs. Estate agents' fees range from 1 per cent to about 3 per cent of the eventual selling price of the property. If you instruct an agent on a 'sole agency' basis (he is the only agent acting for you) the fee will be slightly lower than his normal charge. If you decide to sell through a property shop, charges are made on the registration of the property. In some cases this initial fee is all that is payable, whilst in other cases another fee may be due if a sale is forthcoming. Here again, compare the charges and ask what service will be offered for that charge (full details in Part Two).

Elegant replacement windows bring new character to this attractive bungalow.

ANTICIPATED SELLING PRICE OF EXISTING PROPERTY

This figure is necessary in order to calculate what you can afford when you have another home to sell first. Most estate agents will give you a free verbal assessment of this figure if you are not sure what it is likely to be, but if you require written confirmation they may make a small charge.

REMOVAL COSTS

It's early days yet, but there is no harm in approaching several removal companies and obtaining quotations, or finding out how much it would cost to do it yourself.

A WORD ABOUT DEPOSITS

At the time you exchange contracts, you will be required to pay a 10 per cent deposit — that is 10 per cent of the total purchase price. If you are selling a house in a simultaneous transaction your solicitor may be able to arrange for your buyer's deposit to be passed on towards your own. But do not rely on this! As a purchaser you are usually expected to find the required amount from your own resources. If you do not have the necessary funds readily available, you can arrange a bridging loan through your bank, which your solicitor will pay off on your behalf on completion of the transaction. Don't worry too much about it at this stage. Your solicitor will notify you nearer the time and with his assistance you can make all the necessary arrangements.

Most builders will require a deposit to be lodged on a new house. The amount varies, so make enquiries as you visit each site. Very few estate agents will expect you to leave a deposit on a second-hand property, though some may ask you to do so. Make sure you are given an official signed receipt for any money you leave, and never leave a non-returnable deposit with anyone. Check too what deductions, if any, would be made if the transaction does not complete and the deposit is returned. Any monies deposited are, in reality, part of the total purchase price and the necessary adjustments will be made on completion.

SPECIAL NOTE

If you are unemployed and need to move to a new area to find a job, the Government's Job Search and Employment Transfer Scheme may help with costs. Full details can be obtained from your local Jobcentre.

Once you have all these figures to hand, or at least a fairly accurate assessment of what they are likely to be, you can work out what you can afford to pay for your new house.

If you are wise enough to stay within these limits you will not find yourself in difficulties later on!

Checklist 2 shows how to do this if you are only *buying* a property, but turn to Checklist 3 if you are *buying and selling* a house.

Checklist 2: What can you afford?

1) How to calculate your maximum purchase price when purchasing only:
   The lender says I can borrow: £...............
   The deposit I have saved is: £...............
       Maximum Purchase Price: £...............

2) Other payments will be required for:
   Solicitor's fees (plus VAT): £...............
   Valuation fees (plus VAT): £...............
   Survey fees if required (plus VAT): £...............
   Indemnity policy if required: £...............
   Removal expenses (plus VAT): £...............
       Total expenses: £...............

3) If you are purchasing a new property, don't forget to allow enough money for a deposit to be paid.

4) Check on any extra costs that may be incurred if a top-up loan is anticipated.

5) Allow yourself a small contingency fund for incidentals.

Checklist 3: What can you afford?

1   How to calculate costs for buying and selling.
Expenses:

Outstanding mortgage (including redemption charge)	£...............
Solicitor's fees (buying) plus VAT:	£...............
Solicitor's fees (selling) plus VAT:	£...............
Estate agent's fees or advertising costs plus VAT:	£...............
Survey fees (if required) plus VAT:	£...............
Indemnity policy (if required):	£...............
Valuation fees plus VAT:	£...............
Removal expenses plus VAT:	£...............
Total expenses:	£...............
Value of existing house:	£...............
Cash savings to be contributed:	£...............
Total assets:	£...............
LESS total expenses from above:	£...............
Deposit therefore:	£...............
SO lender says I can borrow:	£...............
plus deposit as above:	£...............
Maximum purchase price:	£...............

2)   If you are purchasing a new property, don't forget to allow enough money for a deposit to be paid.

3)   Check on any extra costs that may be incurred if a top-up loan is anticipated.

4)   Allow yourself a small contingency fund for incidentals.

2 · Choosing the Right Property

Now you have a good idea of the price you can afford to pay for your new home, you can set about the exciting task of finding a property which not only offers the most suitable accommodation in the most convenient area, but is also the best possible value for your money and a sound investment for the future.

Comparing all the houses in your price range is essential if you are to discover which one offers the best value, so register your requirements with all the local estate agents, visit new building developments, scour the 'Houses for Sale' advertisements in local and national newspapers and watch out for 'For Sale' boards. If you make any appointments to view make sure you keep them!

VIEWING NEW PROPERTIES

As a buyer you may well prefer a new house to an older one, but there are often difficulties which may not come immediately to mind. Builders have a nasty habit of not completing the property by the date they promise, and there are often teething troubles such as settlement cracks, noisy plumbing and other minor difficulties. You will probably have to make up the garden from scratch, too, which can be

These attractive starter homes are realistically priced and ideal for first-time buyers.

costly. However, builders are now realising that the commodity they offer must be built to a very high standard if it is to sell well, and they are also introducing more 'extras' into their homes, such as fitted bedroom furniture and fully-equipped kitchens.

Often part-exchange deals are offered in an effort to alleviate the problems and delays caused by long 'chains' of sales and purchases (full details in Part Two). You may consider this a very important argument towards choosing a newly-built house if you have not sold your own property. Builders have grown to appreciate the special problems of first-time buyers and the elderly, and many now offer starter homes and retirement flats at realistic prices. One advantage of buying a new house is that most builders will allow a respectable amount of time in which you can arrange your mortgage and so on, and the plot you have reserved will not be re-offered during that period. However, they will reserve the right to increase the price of the property should building costs rise. Find out all these stipulations before you leave a holding deposit, and make sure you can get it back if the transaction does not complete.

National House Building Council

All reputable builders are registered members of the NHBC, Chiltern Avenue, Amersham, Bucks HP6 5AP, and every house they build will be covered by the Council's ten-year guarantee. The builder himself will be responsible for any defects resulting from his failure to comply with the Council's requirements for the first two years. Thereafter the Council will assume responsibility for any such defect. If the builder should go bankrupt before the two-year period, the Council will pay for the work, though it is often very difficult for the owner to pursue the matter. This is best left in the hands of your solicitor and you may still have to pay up to 10 per cent of the cost yourself.

If you move into a newly-built house, make a careful list of

If you move on to an unfinished site, be prepared for dumpers and diggers to disturb the peace whilst building work continues.

35

Creating a new garden is an expensive undertaking. Be prepared for a great deal of hard work and expense before results like these can be achieved.

all the minor faults as they come to light. During the first six months of occupation most builders will rectify these faults for you.

VIEWING OLDER PROPERTIES

The disadvantages of buying an older house are that decoration is often necessary, maybe even some structural repair work, but you may find that various extras like curtain rails, carpets and similar items that are expensive to replace are already included in the purchase price. If you are buying any second-hand property, especially if it is an older one, refer again to the list of restrictions you discussed with the lender earlier, to ensure that you do not involve yourself with the legal costs of agreeing to buy a property which is not likely to be adequate security for your advance.

Listed Buildings

You cannot demolish or extend any listed building in any way that would change the character of the property without seeking special authorisation from the local authority. Lists of such buildings and conservation areas with properties of special historic and architectural value to which stipulations apply can be obtained from your local authority.

Home Improvement Grants

If you are considering purchasing a property for improvement or renovation, you may be able to receive a local authority grant towards the costs. The property must be freehold, or, in the case of a leasehold property, have several years of the lease still to run. Full details can be obtained from your local authority and are contained in the leaflet *Home Improvement Grants — A Guide for Home-owners, Landlords and Tenants.*

This listed building must not be altered in any way that would change its character or appearance.

THE FINAL CHOICE

There are so many different styles and types of property available that it is impossible to decide what to buy until you have spent some time looking round and comparing, and before you make your final decision be critical! Consider all the bad points the property may have and don't agree to purchase it unless you feel sure you can live with those faults. Checklist 4 indicates some of the more important points to look out for as you view each property. Why not take it with you or jot down details in a notebook? It is very difficult to remember everything once you have left. When it comes to comparisons you may find rating each property from one to ten helpful too!

Checklist 4: Details of properties viewed

1) Is the property in good repair or should you allow for improvements and re-decoration? Take a careful look at ceilings and walls for any signs of extensive cracking or damp. Outside check the roof for missing tiles. Does the chimney look firm? Are there any signs of damage to guttering or down pipes? Check windows and door frames for rotting timber. Pointing should be firm with no major cracks on outside walls.

2) Will the property fit into the category of mortgageable properties the lender discussed with you earlier?

3) Is the accommodation of suitable size?

4) What type of flooring is under the carpet?

5) What fixtures and fittings are *included* in the price?

6) What fixtures and fittings are to be sold separately?

7) What is the main source of heating, i.e. oil-fired central heating, gas-fired central heating, night-storage heaters, solid fuel? Is it all in working order?

8) What are the average running costs of the property? Ask the vendor for a breakdown of gas, electricity, rates, water rates, coal or oil.

9) Where exactly is the boundary? It could be a problem if you have difficult neighbours.

10) Is there a shared driveway or communal area of any kind? This again can cause problems with parking and people walking across your garden. Check details carefully.

11) If so, what are the restrictions, if any?

12) Any other restrictions (known as restrictive covenants)? These are sometimes imposed to restrict the owner from running a business from the property, hanging out washing etc. Your solicitor will find out full details during his enquiries if there are any problems.

13) Is the property likely to be affected by noise or pollution from nearby buildings? Take into account factories, main roads or by-passes, public houses, cafes, restaurants. Consider, too, any petrol station, public sports facilities or other buildings that could cause difficulties with passing traffic or parking. (Stand in the garden and listen for a few minutes — even neighbours can be noisy!)

14) What are the neighbours like? (Many people move because they do not get on with their neighbours, but they are not very likely to admit this to you!)

15) Is there adequate parking space on the premises? (Neighbourhood disagreements often arise because of thoughtless parking.)

16) Is there a septic tank or main drainage?

17) What improvements or extensions have been carried out recently?

18) Has any planning permission been approved in relation to the property and if so what for?

19) Is there a National House Builders Certificate available?

20) If double glazing or cavity wall insulation has been installed, are guarantees available?

21) Will there be vacant possession on completion?

22) If the property is leasehold, check details of the lease:
    a) number of years outstanding (a property will be less valuable if there are only a few years of the lease left to run);
    b) ground rent;
    c) maintenance charges;
    d) other charges.

23) Any other questions.

24) It is wise to visit the property at different times during the day and at weekends to see whether the quiet area you first saw is still just as quiet and pleasant, and that parked cars, children's bikes and ball games are not likely to cause concern during the evenings and holiday periods.

3 · *Making an Offer*

Hopefully by now you will have viewed several different properties within your price range and this will undoubtedly give you valuable information as to what is, and what is not, good value for money, taking into account any fixtures and fittings or other extras that may be included. You may find that these extras give you a basis for any bargaining you may wish to enter into. You will also be in a stronger position to bargain if you can proceed immediately. This means that you must already have arranged a mortgage 'in principle', and if you have a property to sell you must already have found a buyer who has exchanged or is just about to exchange contracts with you. If there is some doubt as to whether you can obtain a mortgage, or if there is likely to be a long delay while the sale of your existing house is tied up, don't be surprised if the seller tells you to come back again when your position has improved. In the meantime he will continue to offer his house for sale in case someone more promising comes along. This applies whether you are dealing through an agent or directly with the vendor. It is important, too, to find out whether the seller can go ahead. You don't want to agree to buy his house only to find he is unable to keep his part of the bargain!

It is very easy to be drawn into negotiations that do not

Warden-assisted retirement homes, with every facility for single or married couples.

complete and all the costs incurred will still have to be paid. So, where 'chains' are concerned, proceed with caution!

GAZUMPING

It is fair to say that most sellers put their house up for sale at the highest possible price, and at times when few similar properties are available it is well to offer a figure as near to the asking price as possible, or you could find another buyer offering a higher figure than your own and the vendor — being only human — accepting that offer. Of course what he should do before accepting an offer from anyone else is to tell you what has happened and give you an opportunity to meet the new figure. If your transaction is well under way, this is obviously the most sensible course of action, but unfortunately many sellers ignore this point and are so pleased to be offered a higher price that they accept it without

42

a second thought; and if their negotiations with you have not yet reached the point where contracts have been exchanged, they have every right to do so!

Once everyone is in a strong position to go ahead, and a price has been agreed and accepted, the arrangements must be confirmed in writing. If an agent is dealing with the sale, you can leave it to him to write to the vendor, the vendor's solicitor, your solicitor, and confirm everything in writing.

PRIVATE SALES

In the case of a private sale, there are several important questions you will need to ask the vendor, the answers to which should be passed on to your solicitor. If you refer to Checklist 5, these questions are listed for you. As you can see, the information relates to the price agreed and details your solicitor will need about the vendor. It also gives the necessary information required by your lender in order that he can arrange for a valuation to be carried out. Pass this information to your solicitor as soon as possible. Also make a comprehensive list of any fixtures and fittings included in the price and a separate list of any additional items you may have agreed to buy, showing the price you have offered for each in case there is a dispute later on. Under no circumstances leave a deposit direct with a vendor. If he insists that you should leave one to show good faith, instruct your solicitor to forward it on your behalf. If you are buying direct from the vendor, the offer should be confirmed in a short letter similar to the following:

Dear [name of seller]
   Re: *[full address of property to be sold]*
Further to my recent visit to the above property, I confirm my offer to purchase of £..............SUBJECT TO CONTRACT

AND SURVEY, and would ask you to instruct your solicitor to issue draft contracts to [name and address of your own solicitor] as soon as possible.

Keep copies of everything for yourself and send further copies to your solicitor for record purposes. 'Subject to contract and survey' means that you are covered if for any

Checklist 5: Details required by purchaser in the event of a private sale (These details should be forwarded direct to your solicitor)

1) Full address of property.
2) Agreed purchase price (subject to contract and survey).
3) Leasehold/freehold: if leasehold, state number of years remaining on lease, ground rent, details of any other charges.
4) Vendor's full name, address (if different from above), telephone number at home and work.
5) Full name, address and telephone number of vendor's solicitor.
6) Has vendor found somewhere to move on to?
7) Is his purchase part of a chain (if so, give full details)?
8) How can you contact him in order to arrange a survey?
9) Make a list of fixtures and fittings included in the purchase price and a separate list of any items you agree to purchase direct, together with the agreed and accepted price for each. Pass these to your solicitor with the above information. Keep a copy for yourself.

To avoid confusion, make a comprehensive list of 'extras', such as carpets, curtains, curtain rails, centre and wall light fittings, to be included in the sale.

This road will not be made up and adopted by the local authority until the site is complete. There could be a retention on the mortgage until this work is carried out.

reason negotiations should fail to reach the exchange of contracts. Until that takes place, either party can withdraw from the transaction.

CONTRACT RACES

If a vendor has two or more people wishing to buy his property, it is possible that he will wish them to enter into a contract race. Each party will then be expected to go through the whole procedure of buying, right up to the exchange of contracts. The first person to sign and exchange the contract will then win the race. If you are drawn into such a situation remember that someone is going to lose the race and it could be *you*. Should this happen you will still have to pay all the legal costs, survey and valuation fees incurred along the way. It is therefore extremely important that you do not enter a contract race unless you stand an excellent chance of winning. Your own house should be sold with contracts ready to exchange, your mortgage approved in principle and your surveyor ready to go. Push your solicitor or conveyancing company into top gear and constantly pester them all until the race is won!

4 · Applying for Your Mortgage

Having been sensible enough to conduct initial enquiries into the possibilities of obtaining a mortgage, you should now be in a position to approach the lender and complete your mortgage application form knowing that it will be considered and there is not likely to be a delay. You should also have decided which type of mortgage to apply for. The valuation fee must be submitted with the application form (a scale of charges will be provided by the lender). If you also want an independent survey to be carried out, now is the time to instruct a chartered surveyor to do this for you.

On receipt of your mortgage application form, your lender will take up references with your employer and, if these are satisfactory, will then arrange for a survey to be carried out. If you are being pressurised to go ahead very quickly, it may be worth asking the lender to do both jobs at once (some do anyway) to hurry things along, but don't forget you could lose your survey fee if by any chance your references are not satisfactory.

Keep in contact with the seller and ask him to let you know when the surveyor for the lender has called. This will give you some indication as to how fast things are moving and will show the seller that you are doing your utmost to purchase his house!

A larger four-bedroomed house suitable for a growing family, chosen for its close proximity to schools and local amenities.

YOUR MORTGAGE OFFER

It is always a great relief when you finally receive the long-awaited mortgage offer, but before you sign and accept it read it through very carefully. Make sure you understand all the terms and conditions stipulated and that you agree with the figures, especially where adjustments have been made for insurance premiums. If you have any queries at all, or the figures do not seem to be consistent with those you expected, pop along to the lender or your solicitor and ask for an explanation. Don't sign and return the form until you are completely satisfied.

RETENTIONS

If the property to be mortgaged does not meet the standard required by the lender, he may stipulate that certain works must be carried out and will hold back (retain) a portion of

Older terraced houses, individually modernised, demonstrating what can be achieved if you buy an older property.

the advance, usually an amount he considers the work will cost, until this work has been done to his satisfaction and the property offers the security required. He will provide full details of the work and it will then be up to you to arrange for it to be undertaken. In most cases you can obtain bridging finance to cover the costs. You will then have to pay another survey fee for a final inspection and, if the work is acceptable, the money retained will be released to you.

DOWN-VALUATIONS

A surveyor may consider that the property is 'over-priced' for the security it offers, in which case he will 'down-value' it, and your mortgage will be adjusted accordingly.

WITHDRAWING FROM A DEAL

If you decide to withdraw from the deal altogether because of the problems that have come to light, don't forget that the costs so far will still have to be paid. An alternative may be to re-negotiate a lower purchase price with the seller or his agent, pointing out the difficulties. There is certainly no harm in contacting the seller to discuss the problems and get his reaction.

PRIVATELY-BUILT HOUSES

If you own your own piece of land and wish to have a house built to your own specification on it, most lenders will advance stage payments as the work progresses. Plans must be submitted to the lender and you will have to pay a survey fee for each stage to be inspected before the advance is forthcoming.

5 · Exchanging the Contract

The period between agreeing to buy a house and exchange of contracts is a very frustrating one. You will probably feel in a state of limbo, anxious to get on with things but unable to do so until everyone else has played his part. At any point until contracts have been exchanged, either party can withdraw from the transaction, but once exchange has taken place the matter becomes legally binding, and if you should then fail to complete you will forfeit your deposit and also have to pay any costs incurred by the seller. If the seller should fail to complete, you can ask a court to order him to do so and to compensate you for any money you have lost.

Should you have received a mortgage offer and then for some reason the purchase does not proceed, the offer can be transferred to another property. It will be necessary for the lender to value the next property you choose, just as before, and another fee will be payable. It is well to check that funds are still available too. If you are unable to take up the first amount allocated to you, and there are more people waiting for mortgages, you could be put back to the end of the queue again, and may end up waiting several months for the money to come through.

THE CONTRACT

The draft contract will probably have passed between the two solicitors several times before your solicitor finally approves it, but once he has completed his enquiries and made sure there are no legal difficulties relating to the house, you will be asked to read it through with him for approval and signature.

Try to arrange, with the help of your solicitor, for everyone involved in your chain (if there is one) to agree on a completion date. If this can be co-ordinated properly at this stage, it could save a great many problems later on.

Your contract will include the following details:

1) Buyer's name, address and occupation. Seller's name, address and occupation.

2) A full description of the property and its location.

3) Whether leasehold or freehold. If leasehold, full details of the lease, its charges, terms and conditions.

4) Details of any 'easements' such as rights of way, rights of drainage and sewage. Read these through very carefully to make sure you understand all the details.

5) Full details of any other restrictions appertaining to the property and its land. Make sure you know exactly what they are.

6) The full purchase price.

7) The completion date.

8) Interest to be charged on any unpaid money or delayed completion.

9) Capacity in which the seller offers the property, i.e. owner, mortgagee, trustee, executor of a will.

10) The use of the property, e.g. a family home.

11) A list of the items included in the purchase price and a list of the items to be purchased separately and the agreed price.

12) Title number of the property as per land registry (if registered).

13) Vacant possession, i.e. the property will be completely empty on completion.

It is very important that you understand all the details relating to boundaries, rights of way, leases, shared amenities, parking rights and so on, so don't be afraid to ask your solicitor to clarify any points which seem ambiguous or unclear — this will be your last opportunity to do so.

Incorporated in the contract will also be certain 'conditions of sale', which are standard rules that remain unchanged. However, make sure you know what they are.

Only sign the contract when you are quite happy with all its terms and conditions.

JOINT OWNERSHIP

When two people purchase the house or flat jointly, they may wish to enter into a 'joint tenancy'. Here neither can sell his share of the property without the other's full agreement, and should one person die the property will automatically pass to the other partner. Many married couples prefer this arrangement as it offers security for both partners.

The second choice is a 'tenancy in common', where both parties can dispose of their share in the home as they choose, perhaps by leaving their share to a son or daughter in the event of their death. This system is often chosen by unmarried couples who wish to retain their independence.

THE DEPOSIT

A 10 per cent deposit will now have to be paid. Where your purchase is co-ordinating with the sale of your existing house, the cheque you pass on could be greatly reduced if your solicitor has been able to arrange for your buyer's deposit to

Unusual executive homes forming part of a new marina village.

be used towards your own, or he has been clever enough to persuade your seller to accept a lower deposit. There will be two copies of the contract drawn up, one to be signed by the seller and one to be signed by yourself. When your signed copy and deposit has been accepted by the seller, and his signed copy accepted by you (or your respective solicitors) the exchange has taken place and the transaction at last becomes legally binding.

Don't think that contracts have been exchanged just because you have signed your part of the contract and left a cheque with your solicitor. If there are difficulties further along the chain he could hold on to it for several days until the problems are resolved. So keep in contact with him to find out exactly what is happening.

6 · Preparing for Completion

Completion usually takes place about four weeks after exchange, during which time your solicitor or conveyancing company will be completing the paperwork. During this interim period there is a great deal you will need to do, too. Arrangements for the move must be made. The easiest, though more costly, method is to employ a removal company to do all the hard work for you. You can even arrange for them to do your packing! If you don't want to go that far, ask them to deliver several packing cases a few days before the move and pack all your personal belongings and breakable items carefully yourself. Where necessary, mark crates and packing cases 'Handle With Care' or 'This Way Up', and so on. A lot of time will be saved if each packing case is also marked with a list of its contents and the room it is destined for.

Removal companies who are members of the British Association of Removers, 279 Gray's Inn Road, London WC1X 85Y, will provide helpful leaflets, so it is worth choosing a removal firm that is a member. Charges vary quite considerably and will depend a great deal on the amount to be moved and the length of the journey to be undertaken. So, if you haven't already done so, ask for estimates from several different companies.

This self-drive van is the most popular size for 'do-it-yourself' removals (courtesy Avis Rent-a-Car).

For the really brave and exceptionally sturdy, the alternative is to hire a van and do it yourself! This will be made a lot easier if you are able to hire a van large enough to move everything in one go (you can drive a vehicle up to the weight of 7.5 tonnes laden weight on an ordinary driving licence). Enlist the help of friends and relatives, be ready with endless cans of liquid refreshment and give someone the task of providing fish and chips for lunch — you probably won't have the time to stop and eat! It *is* hard work, but it will probably be cheaper. Hire charges can be based on a fixed sum per day or week with unlimited mileage or a smaller fixed sum plus a mileage charge. It will be necessary to leave a deposit when you hire the van, and don't forget to check on the conditions of insurance should the van be damaged during the hire period.

Checklist 6 shows some of the more important jobs that must also be done. You will find it helpful if you are not sure where to begin.

On completion day itself, you will need to know where to collect the keys for your new home, so find out from the seller where he intends to leave them for collection, and also find out what time of the day your solicitor anticipates the formalities to be concluded, because until that time you are not entitled to have the keys or take possession of the property. You are not entitled to move anything at all into the property until completion. Carpets should not be delivered or fitted, nor should domestic appliances be installed. If there really is no alternative, make the necessary arrangements via your solicitor, who will organise the matter officially on your behalf.

Checklist 6: Getting ready for completion day

1) Arrange for a removal van.
2) If the removal company are not packing for you, collect crates and boxes for packing.
3) Make sure each crate or box is clearly marked with a list of its contents and the room to which it should be delivered. Where necessary mark 'This Way Up' or 'Handle With Care'.
4) Arrange for gas/electric meters to be read at your existing property the day you move out.
5) Arrange for gas fitters/electricians to disconnect cookers etc and re-install at the new premises.
6) Check that the vendor has made the necessary arrangements for his meters to be read at the new property (you don't want to pay for his gas or electricity!). (All this can be done at your local gas/electricity showroom.)

Checklist 6: Getting ready for completion day

7) Contact British Telecom and make the necessary arrangements for a disconnection and reconnection at the new property.

8) Complete a change of address form at the local post office so that any mail sent to your old address will be forwarded on to you.

9) Advise your bank, H.P. companies, friends etc of your new address and from what date.

10) Contact the vendor and find out where you can collect the keys on the day of completion.

11) Keep some thick paper, or old rugs, handy to cover floors when moving out and moving in.

12) Arrange for milk deliveries to your new home and be sure to cancel your present delivery.

13) Allow for refuse collections.

14) Make suitable provision for your children and pets.

15) Remember that a freezer is easier to move if it is empty.

16) Arrange for suitable insurance for the contents of your home as from the day you move in, and if necessary arrange a suitable cover for any breakages or damage during the move itself.

17) If you are moving out of a property leave it clean and tidy, and don't leave rubbish and debris for the next occupant to deal with.

RATES

Rates and water rates are usually paid in advance, which means that the seller will probably have paid a certain portion of rates beyond the date he is due to move out. If this is the case he can claim a rebate from the rating authority or from yourself. As the new occupant you will be responsible for the payment of rates as from the day you move in. Check that your solicitor has arranged these details for you. For a limited period, usually three months, rates are not payable on an empty house or on uninhabitable property in the course of refurbishment.

BRIDGING LOANS

Banks are able to provide bridging loans to enable you to complete your purchase should your sale and your purchase not tie up successfully. However, they will be reluctant to advance an 'open-ended' amount and will probably require proof that a contract is available on the pending sale. Interest rates are usually high and this step is not recommended unless you can adequately afford the costs and there is no alternative option open to you.

THE COMPLETION

The property does not become yours until completion of the transaction takes place. Your solicitor will pay the outstanding monies due, on receipt of which the seller's solicitor will hand over the title deed including the transfer (or conveyance) which will be kept by your lender as security for the mortgage. If the title is registered it will be forwarded to the land registry for a new entry to be made. If you are buying the house outright and no mortgage is required, the relevant documents will be sent directly to you.

When all these formalities are complete, the property finally becomes yours.

PROBLEMS WITH MORTGAGE REPAYMENTS

Should you be made redundant, or perhaps have a long illness which makes it difficult for you to keep up your mortgage payments, it is very important that you contact the lender *before* your repayments fall into arrears. In today's difficult financial times, there are very few building societies or banks who will not lend a sympathetic ear and agree to make a temporary adjustment suited to your circumstances. In some cases the lender may agree to reduce your monthly repayments and lengthen the term of the loan to compensate, or he may allow you to pay the interest only for the time being. It is more difficult if an endowment mortgage is taken on and you should therefore contact your insurance company and the lender as soon as there is any likelihood of your repayments falling behind.

The lender is perfectly entitled to repossess your house if payments are heavily in arrears, and he will almost certainly do so if you are not prepared to discuss your difficulties with him and try to reach a mutually acceptable solution.

7 · Buying by Auction

Where a house is to be sold by auction, all the preparation work must be done by the time you begin your bidding. If your bid is accepted at the auction, you will have to pay a 10 per cent deposit right away and sign a binding contract which records the sale.

1) Obtain the auctioneer's written particulars of the property and view it in the usual way, making careful notes of its condition and any extras to be included in the sale.
2) Instruct your solicitor to proceed with searches etc and check the conditions mentioned in the particulars.
3) If you require a mortgage, apply for one in the usual way. You will need a firm mortgage offer when your bid is accepted. If a bridging loan for the 10 per cent deposit is required, now is the time to arrange it.
4) Instruct a surveyor to carry out a full report. This is extremely important if the property is an old or unusual one, as properties put to auction often are.
5) Make sure you know exactly what the property is worth before you put in a bid, and don't exceed the amount you can afford.

All this preparation will inevitably result in fees having to be paid, and it will be money lost if your bid is not accepted.

Sometimes auctioneers will accept 'tenders' (written offers) for the property prior to auction, and if your tender is accepted you are obliged to proceed with the purchase.

As you can see it is extremely important that you conduct matters up to the point of exchange of contracts *before* the auction, or you could face a very difficult situation if your bid is accepted and you are not ready.

PART TWO: SELLING YOUR PROPERTY

The inevitable question arises — to sell first or buy first? The answer is really quite simple. If you are relying on the proceeds from your existing house or flat to purchase a new one, you must find a buyer before you can complete a purchase. It therefore follows that as soon as you decide the time has come to move you should put your house on the market and line someone up as a buyer as soon as you can. If you haven't found another property to buy, explain this to your prospective purchaser, and it is then up to him to choose whether to wait, or to buy elsewhere. The secret is to co-ordinate both your sale and your purchase very carefully. You are not legally bound to either until contracts have been exchanged, therefore you don't want to sign away your existing house without having another one to move into (unless you have sufficient money to buy it outright); neither do you want to commit yourself to a purchase without having a buyer for your own house (unless again, you have sufficient funds readily available to do so).

This decided, you must now choose whether to sell your house yourself or instruct a selling agent to do so for you.

8 · Choosing a Selling Agent

There are a number of options open to you if you decide to enlist the services of a selling agent. You can choose from the following or use them all!

CONVENTIONAL ESTATE AGENTS

An estate agent's fee will be payable to the agent who introduces the buyer who completes the transaction. These fees allow for a 'no sale, no fee' condition. As mentioned in Part One, fees range from 1 to 3 per cent of the eventual selling price, but are usually lower if you instruct only one agent on a sole agency basis. This means he is the only agent acting on your behalf. However, your chances of selling will probably be increased if you instruct several different agents.

Sometimes agents act jointly on a sale. This is an arrangement they make between each other, perhaps because the first agent you instruct feels he cannot offer the best service as his office is too far away from the property. He would then sub-instruct another agent in your immediate vicinity to act jointly with him. If a sale is forthcoming, one fee only will be payable to the main agent, who will split it with the sub-agent under the terms they have agreed. To eliminate the 'cowboys' from the profession, the National

A home centre within a large store, offering comprehensive financial and legal facilities to its customers, in addition to its selling service (courtesy Home Centre, Debenhams, Southampton).

Association of Estate Agents, Arbon House, 21 Jury Street, Warwick CV34 4EH, has set down strict codes of conduct for its members, and any agent you instruct should be a bonded member of that organisation.

PROPERTY SHOPS AND COMPUTER SALES

This type of house sales service is growing rapidly and is certainly cheaper. You pay a registration fee as soon as you place your house on their register — which will of course be lost if a sale is not forthcoming. In some cases this is the only fee payable, whilst in others another fee becomes due if a sale is negotiated. Some property shops will simply put you in touch with prospective buyers and leave the rest to you, whilst others now offer a comprehensive service to compete with estate agents, and the resulting competition in respect of fees must be good for the consumer.

SOLICITORS

The Law Society has recently given permission for its members to act as selling agents. Fees and the service offered will be entirely dependent upon the method in which solicitors choose to take up this option. Your solicitor will give you all the details on request if he is acting in this capacity.

BUILDING SOCIETIES

Proposed new legislation is likely to allow building societies to act as selling agents too. This may not take effect until 1987 and details will be available at that time.

PART-EXCHANGE

The problems of selling a house and co-ordinating the sale with a purchase can be greatly relieved if you are hoping to buy a new property and the builder is offering a part-exchange arrangement. Your existing house will have to be less expensive than the one you want to buy, and the builder will instruct a local estate agent to value your house on his behalf. He will then offer you a price based on that figure which is usually between 90 and 95 per cent of the valuation. If this figure is acceptable, he will purchase the house to leave you free to buy his. He will then put the old house back on the market for re-sale. This is a very convenient way of avoiding the chain situation, but do make sure you receive a fair figure for your old house. If you feel you could get more and still complete the transaction in time, sell your house in the usual way.

9 · The Service an Estate Agent Offers

If you decide to instruct an estate agent to act on your behalf, you should choose one whose office is situated in the same area as the property. He will know the current selling value of your house and have an intimate knowledge of the competition. This puts him in a strong position to value your house accurately. The main advantage of selling through an agent is that he will already have a register of applicants to refer to, maybe even one who is particularly looking for a house like yours, in which case he will contact that applicant immediately and circulate the particulars of your property to everyone else on his register. Many sales are tied up in this way, often before the property is advertised in local newspapers.

You are perfectly entitled to engage as many selling agents as you choose, which should improve your chances of finding a buyer quickly. However, too many agents can confuse the matter, and it will then be very much up to you to keep every agent informed of exactly what is going on at any one time. It puts an agent — and yourself — in a very embarrassing position if he has a prospective viewer in his office, rings you to make an appointment, and is promptly told that the house was sold two weeks ago by someone else! A more precise hold can be kept on the situation if you instruct only one agent to

'For Sale' boards invite enquiries from prospective purchasers. However, too many boards may give the impression that the house is difficult to sell.

act for you on a sole-agency basis, which will also be cheaper. But make sure you set a limit on the period the sole agency covers, so that if you are not happy with the service provided you can instruct another agent (fees will then revert to the normal rate).

BOARDS

Too many 'For Sale' boards in one garden tend to give prospective buyers the impression that the house is difficult to sell and therefore something is wrong with it. So, if you agree to have a board erected, only have one! A board is certainly a good advertisement for the selling agent and will draw attention to the fact that your house is for sale, so encouraging people to enquire further. Have a 'view strictly by appointment' ticket attached to the board if you are concerned about people hammering on your door unannounced.

ADVERTISING

The efficiency of the estate agent will be reflected in the way he advertises. A dust-free, up-to-date window display with no faded photographs or dead flies is essential, as is an eye-catching advertisement in local and national newspapers, hopefully including photographs of the house advertised. If you don't see your house there — find out why! If you are not impressed with the agent's advertising methods, a prospective buyer certainly won't be, nor will he be tempted to venture into a scruffy office strewn with empty coffee cups and filled with cigarette smoke. So be careful which agent you choose!

THE SPECIFICATION

The specification of your house must be perfect in every respect. It must be presented in a first-class manner — no spelling mistakes or inky splodges from copying or duplicating machines — and have a clear colour photograph prominently displayed. Before you allow the final specification to be handed out, read it through very carefully and check that it is correct down to the last detail.

Never include items that you do not intend to leave in the property. Carpets and curtains and other extras mentioned on the specification should be *included* in the price and not *added* to the value of the house itself. If you want to sell such things separately, supply a full list for ease of reference and to avoid any misunderstanding later.

As soon as you instruct an agent and the property has been measured up and full details taken, the agent will confirm everything in writing to you, setting out the fees and the terms of your agreement with him. It is then his job to find a buyer who can complete the purchase of your property to coincide successfully with any purchase you are making.

Ask the agent to accompany all viewers if you feel unhappy about showing people round yourself, and if you leave keys with an agent make sure he reports to you each time he takes someone to look round. If you have left a key with an agent, he must of course escort all viewers and not hand them your key to view on their own — even if you have moved out and the house is empty.

10 · The Negotiations

You are employing an agent to act for you in your best interest and to get the highest possible price for your property. With this in mind you must leave it to him to negotiate prices with any prospective buyers. Very often a buyer will make it clear as soon as he views the house that he wishes to purchase. He may well discuss figures in general with you, but you should refer him to the agent in order that a firm offer can be negotiated. The agent will already know, or will certainly check, the following details:

1) Whether the applicant can obtain a mortgage.
2) If the applicant has a house to sell, whether the sale is well under way.
3) Whether the applicant can meet with your requirements regarding completion.

The agent will also conclude negotiations for any extras such as carpets, curtains, bathroom fittings etc.

If the applicant seems in a very strong position to complete the transaction, the agent will confirm everything in writing on your behalf to your solicitor and yourself, the buyer and to his solicitor. Should the applicant require assistance with his mortgage arrangements, the agent will be able to help and can also give advice on surveys.

FOLLOWING THROUGH

Once the sale is under way, your agent will monitor progress very carefully indeed, checking with other agents and solicitors on the continued progress of your buyer's chain (if there is one) and making sure that his mortgage is arranged satisfactorily. If at any time there appears to be a delay or problems of any kind, your agent will contact you and advise you to continue offering the property to line someone else up as a buyer should the first person not be in a position to continue. You can leave it up to the agent to explain the situation to the first buyer, warning him that, as he is not progressing as planned, should someone more promising come along his offer would supersede any other. If the person wishing to buy your house is not in a strong position to do so, but could be later on, perhaps when his own house is sold, your agent will advise you to keep your property on the market. He will not take your house off his register, or instruct solicitors to begin the legal work, unless he feels there is very little doubt that the sale will complete.

It cannot be stressed enough how important it is to keep in contact with your agent and your solicitor during this interim period. If you are buying another house you will be anxious to co-ordinate the two transactions very carefully, and so it is very important to know exactly what everyone else involved is doing, and to pass on to your agent any information you may have in order that he can follow through your sale to co-ordinate with your purchase. It is often the lack of efficient and friendly liaison which is the cause of problems and misunderstandings. *So keep in touch!*

Should you have instructed more than one agent, don't forget to let the others know what is happening too, and if the house needs to be re-offered ring them all and instruct them to get on with it without delay!

Finally, you can leave your keys with an agent to hand over

to the buyer on completion day. He will not allow the buyer to take possession of the key, however, until he has checked with your solicitor that the money has been received for the property and that legal completion has taken place. An agent's bill is usually accounted for in your solicitor's completion statement. If not, be prepared to pay a separate amount for this.

It is sad to say that not all agents are as efficient as they should be, so, if you are not happy with the service you receive and it does not cover every aspect it should, instruct someone else or consider refusing to pay the full fee he is charging!

11 · Conducting a Private Sale

Selling your house yourself will of course save you a great deal of money. If you wish to sell privately you should not instruct an estate agent at the same time. This can lead to a great deal of confusion and difficulty over the agent's fee. However, if you have already instructed an estate agent but later decide to sell privately, remember that the agent is entitled to his commission, and will certainly claim it, if your eventual purchaser was introduced — however briefly — to your property through that agent. Therefore, once you receive callers you must check whether or not they have registered with the agent involved. If they have not, then all is well and a private sale can be negotiated, but if they have registered then they must conduct any negotiations through the agent. In any event, make a note of the name, address and telephone number of each viewer, should there be a query at a later date. If you have previously had a 'For Sale' board erected by the agent, ask him to remove it. It is very difficult to prove a private sale if the agent's board is clearly advertising that the property is available.

GETTING THE PRICE RIGHT

It is most important when selling your house privately that you arrive at the correct asking price. Too high and no one will buy, too low and you will always regret it! Of course the easiest way is to arrange for a local estate agent or valuer to value the house for you, although he will no doubt charge a modest fee if you intend to sell privately. Alternatively, to assess the value yourself, you can compare the prices of propeties for sale in your area which are of a similar design to your own. Keep an eye on local advertisements and the estate agent's window and familiarise yourself with current market trends. Establish an average asking price for properties like your own and in the same area. If your house has nothing extra to offer than those advertised, simply stick to that figure, but if your property has much more, say an extension, large plot, double glazing etc, then add a little without going far in excess of the competition, or again you will have difficulty in selling. Allow, too, a small amount for negotiation, but make sure this does not push the price up too far. If you are leaving carpets, curtains and other items in the house, make sure they are *included* in the price and not *added* to the value of the property itself. Remember that your purchaser will be arranging a mortgage on the house, not on the items of furniture and sundries in it.

If you have a property which is of an individual nature, then comparisons may be difficult and it would be wise to enlist the help of a valuer or estate agent to ascertain its correct value.

Now ask yourself if you would buy your house today at the figure you have arrived at. If not — why not? Remember that any property is only worth what someone is prepared to pay for it, and buyers know what they want and what they can afford. If your house is over-priced for what it offers, you will have great difficulty selling, so make sure the asking price is as accurate as possible.

Advertise your property in local and national newspapers. *Exchange & Mart* provides the widest possible national coverage.

Fixtures and fittings

Once again we come back to our lists! Draw up a list of the items you intend to leave *included* in the purchase price and a separate list of the items you wish to sell privately. Have these ready to discuss with prospective purchasers when they arrive.

ADVERTISING

Once you have decided on an asking price for your property, the next step is to choose the best method of advertising. Local and national newspapers will probably be your first choice, so ring them and ask for details of their advertising charges, and if your property is visually appealing, and you can possibly afford it, consider advertising with an accompanying photograph. Your advertisement must be accurate, whilst at the same time emphasising the best features of the property. For instance, don't say 'in excellent decorative order' if it is not, or 'in quiet road' if it is on the edge of a motorway, but if it stands in a larger than average plot — say so!

Before drafting your advertisement, spend some time analysing the composition of those listed in the paper you intend to advertise in. Draft out two or three separate advertisements before choosing the final one, and make sure your advertisement goes into the paper the evening you intend to stay in.

DEALING WITH ENQUIRIES

Have a notepad and pen ready by the telephone together with a brief description of the property and the sizes of each room. Before you give anyone your full address, make a note of his name, address and telephone number. Then begin by giving the general location of the property. If your caller still sounds interested, go on to give all the relevant information, but don't give your full address unless your caller wants to make an appointment to view the property. Unfortunately the private seller is often pestered by callers who are just being 'nosey' and who have no intention of buying anything at all. If your caller is genuinely interested in property such as yours he will not object to giving you his name and address, and this is by far the best method to determine who is genuine and who is just wasting your time.

Keep the list of names and addresses for future reference, and don't forget to write down the times when each viewer will be calling.

When there is no response

If you receive no enquiries at all, it could be that your advertisement is inadequate or more probably that the price is too high. A house will always sell if it is correctly priced for its age and condition, so if you don't receive any enquiries at all and you have advertised more than once, changing the wording on each occasion, it could well be that the asking price is excessive. So try re-advertising at a lower figure.

Buying and selling houses is traditionally a seasonal affair. Spring and summer are usually the active times on the property market, whilst Christmas and New Year can often be very stagnant.

There are many other factors which affect the buoyancy of the market too, for instance a change in mortgage interest rates and the availability of mortgage funds. All these factors must be taken into account when analysing the response to your advertisement. The secret is never to be too disappointed if your property does not sell immediately. Just remember that if the price is right your house *will* sell, even if it does take a little longer than you would have wished.

SHOWING PEOPLE ROUND

Greet your viewer with a smile! Check your list and make sure you call him by name. Let him go into each room first and stand just outside or stay by the door. Point out all the special features and answer questions as accurately as possible. It is hoped that your property will be shown at its very best, but if it needs decorating don't make excuses and promise to do it later — if you were going to, it should have been finished by now and will only give your viewer an excuse to offer you a lower price.

Have ready your most recent gas, electricity and rates bills together with any other bills appertaining to the house to give

The first impression a prospective buyer will have, is of your hallway. That impression *must* be a good one.

your viewer an idea of running costs. Be prepared to point out where the property is situated in relation to schools, hospitals, public transport and other amenities and make sure you know exactly where the boundary lies, especially if you are involved in a shared drive or other shared amenity. Make it quite clear which items are included in the price and which items you intend to sell separately.

THE NEGOTIATIONS

Hopefully it will not be long before you find a purchaser willing and able to proceed, but always be prepared to negotiate the final price. Most people make offers lower than the asking price, but seem to think they can get away with very low offers to vendors who are selling privately.

If you can afford to drop slightly and your purchaser is in a strong position to proceed, then it is worth negotiating with him. Equally, if there is a great deal of maintenance work outstanding and you have not already allowed for this in your price, be prepared to negotiate a more realistic figure which accounts for the outstanding work. Don't forget your fixtures and fittings either. Go through your list of items for sale with the prospective purchaser and be ready to barter! Make a note of the prices agreed and keep your lists readily available, as they will be needed later on.

You should now have an agreed and accepted purchase price for the property and an agreed and accepted price for any items to be sold separately, but before you can safely take your property off the open market and instruct your solicitor to issue draft contracts to your purchaser you must be sure that your interested party is in a strong position to reach completion and will not withdraw from the deal at a later date.

Unfortunately it is always very difficult to predict exactly how the transaction will progress once it is under way, but if you take all the necessary precautions right from the beginning, you will certainly reduce the chance of disappointment later on.

Checklist 7: Questions to ask your proposed purchaser to ascertain his purchasing capability

1) Can he provide cash for the purchase?
2) Is he a first-time buyer?
3) If he requires a mortgage:
   a) Has he arranged a mortgage in principle?
   b) Will the advance be readily available on application?
   c) Don't forget that, if the condition of your property is poor, or your home is of an older or unusual construction, your purchaser is unlikely to be able to borrow a high percentage of the purchase price, so ask him if he requires a high mortgage or only a minimal amount.
4). If he has an existing property, is it currently for sale?
   If so has he exchanged contracts on the sale? If not:
   a) Has he found any buyer at all?
   b) Has that buyer sold his own property?
   c) Has that buyer received a mortgage offer?
   d) Has that buyer exchanged contracts on his own sale? If not, how far advanced is the transaction?
   (Make sure you obtain full details of the chain involved beyond your purchaser.)

5) Can your purchaser proceed so that the transaction runs simultaniously with any purchase you are making? If not, ask why and remember that any hold-up on your sale could cause you to lose the house you hope to purchase.

6) If your purchaser is ready to proceed without delay, can you complete your own purchase accordingly?

7) Is there a completion date your purchaser has in mind?

Can your purchaser proceed?

Of course the ideal purchaser for your house will be one who has already exchanged contracts on the sale of his own house, or is a first-time buyer with his mortgage arranged in principle. However, in practice, you will be extemely lucky to find such an ideal person.

It is therefore essential, in order to avoid problems later, that you ascertain exactly what position the person willing to buy your property is in. This is even more crucial if there is more than one interested party, for you must ensure that the person in the best position to complete the transaction is the one you agree to sell to, giving the other first refusal in the event of a breakdown of negotiations.

If you are able to answer 'Yes' to all of the questions appertaining to your proposed purchaser as set out in Checklist 7, then there is no reason why you should not instruct your solicitor to issue draft contracts to that purchaser. If there are a few questions to which the answer is

'No', then you must assume that there will be delays and you should keep your house on the market. Make it clear that although you note the interest which has been shown you still intend offering your property for sale, and if some-one else wishes to buy who is in a better position to proceed, you will have no alternative but to sell to that person. In the meantime, if your first interested party should improve his situation, let him advise you accordingly so that you can negotiate further if the property is still available. Do not instruct your solicitor to issue draft contracts to anyone until they are in the strongest possible position to go ahead, and even then continue to draw up a short-list of other interested parties to fall back on in the event of a breakdown of negotiations.

If you have more than one person willing to purchase and in a strong purchasing position, there is no reason why you should not ask your solicitor to issue draft contracts to both parties as long as everyone is in full agreement. However, contract races such as these are not recommended unless you really have no alternative.

Should you receive a higher offer for your house *after* you have agreed to sell to someone, you should give your first purchaser the opportunity to raise his offer to meet the new one. If the matter has been under way for some time you are both likely to have incurred legal costs and your purchaser will certainly have paid for survey fees and so on, so don't dismiss him too lightly. Tell him what has happened and ask him if he can meet the new offer. If he is unable to do so, then you are quite at liberty to accept the second offer, withdraw the first contract and start all over again, but you will be extremely unpopular and could run the risk of losing both buyers.

Checklist 8: Details required about your purchaser to be forwarded to your solicitor

1) Purchaser's full name.
2) Purchaser's full postal address.
3) Purchaser's telephone number, home and business.
4) Purchaser's solicitor.
5) Full address of property to be sold.
6) Agreed purchase price subject to contract and survey.
7) Leasehold/freehold (give full details if leasehold).
8) From which lender will your purchaser obtain a mortgage?
9) What percentage of the purchase price does he need to borrow?
10) Has he a mortgage already arranged in principle?
11) Is there likely to be any delay in the mortgage advance?
12) Has your purchaser a house to sell?
13) Has he exchanged contracts on his sale? If not, give full details of any chain in which your purchaser is involved.
14) Is your purchaser a first-time buyer?
15) Anticipated completion date.
16) Does your purchaser require a private survey?
17) Can your purchaser complete the transaction in time for any purchase you are making yourself?

Note: Send your solicitor a copy of the list of fixtures and fittings included in the price, and the list of items you have agreed to sell separately together with the price arranged. Take a copy for yourself and one for your purchaser.

Confirming the sale in writing

Once you have found a suitable purchaser and the purchase price has been agreed and accepted, you must ask him the questions set out on Checklist 8. Let your solicitor have these details and also confirm the arrangement to your purchaser in a letter similar to the following.

Dear [name of purchaser]
       Re: [full address of property]
I confirm my acceptance of your offer of £.......................
SUBJECT TO CONTRACT AND SURVEY for the purchase of the above property. My solicitor is [full name and address of your solicitor] and I confirm that I have today instructed him to deal with the conveyance on my behalf. I would ask you to keep me fully informed of your progress at all times and look forward to reaching a satisfactory completion of the transaction.

Keep a copy for yourself and pass another copy on to your solicitor for his records.

Keeping in touch

From now on it is important that you keep in close contact with your purchaser and your solicitor, checking all the time that everything is progressing well. If you are in any doubt, re-offer your property without delay, but ensure that all parties are advised of this action. Check that any purchase you are making is progressing simultaneously.

Your purchaser has no legal access to your house until completion takes place, so don't allow carpets to be fitted, furniture to be moved in, or any household appliances to be installed prior to that date unless there is no alternative. In which case, ask your solicitor to deal with the matter on your behalf.

EXCHANGE AND COMPLETION

Prior to the exchange of contracts you will receive a list of questions relating to the house, which is part of enquiries your buyer's solicitors will be making on his behalf. Answer them as accurately as you can to avoid any queries later on.

The contract appertaining to the house you are selling will have to be signed and your solicitor will be careful to co-ordinate exchange of contracts on your sale with exchange on

Where built-in kitchen appliances are included in the sale, leave them in good, clean working order.

your purchase. Your buyer will pay his 10 per cent deposit in the usual way and, when contracts have been exchanged, all parties are legally bound to complete the transaction.

The final transfer document will also require your signature. Your solicitor will send the buyer's solicitor a 'completion statement' showing how much money must be paid at the time of completion. On completion day itself this amount will be paid to your solicitor who will hand over the deeds to the buyer's solicitor. Once this is done the house is sold and you can hand the keys over to the new buyer.

After the legal fees (and estate agent's fees where applicable) have been paid, your solicitor will pass on any balance remaining.

Don't forget to leave the house clean and tidy for the new occupant and don't remove or change any of the extras you agreed to leave behind.

Appendix: Buying a Property in Scotland

The legal system in Scotland is different from that in England and Wales. You can obtain details of properties for sale from solicitors, property centres and estate agents, though solicitors are more active in the field than estate agents and you will find that most viewing arrangements are made through the solicitors acting for the seller.

Offers on properties in Scotland are usually expected to be higher than the price advertised, although in some cases lower offers may be considered. Once you have seen a property you like, you should tell your solicitor in order that he can register your interest with the other side. You must then arrange for a mortgage and have an adequate survey carried out, basing your offer on that survey. If these steps are favourable, your solicitor will make an official offer in writing for you. This will be set out in a document similar to a draft contract in England and will include a date you wish to move in, how much you are prepared to pay and what contents you wish to buy.

This offer will be considered with any other offer the seller has received. Often a date is fixed by which time all the offers must have been submitted. If your offer is considered, the terms will be negotiated between your solicitor and the seller's solicitor, but once it has been accepted and an acceptance letter has been received, the matter becomes binding. The contract in Scotland is called 'missives'. Once missives have been concluded satisfactorily, the conveyance takes a few weeks to reach completion (called settlement) at which point the purchase money is handed over in return for the keys of the property.

Glossary of Legal Terms

Completion	Payment of purchase monies in exchange for title deeds and keys.
Completion statement	Statement of account showing monies payable by purchaser to complete the transaction.
Contract	Written agreement between buyer and seller committing them to complete the sale or purchase.
Conveyance	Document transferring ownership of land from seller to buyer.
Draft contracts	Suggested content of contract for approval by solicitors prior to final document being drawn up.
Easements	Rights of way etc over neighbouring property.
Freehold	Absolute ownership of property.
Ground rent	Rent paid (usually per annum) for lease.
Leasehold	Property or land held under a lease for a period of years. Tenure by which that property or land is held.
Local searches	Forms sent to local authorities requesting details of any plans that are likely to affect the property or its land.

Mortgage	The legal document assigning property as security for a loan.
Preliminary enquiries	Questions asked by buyer's solicitor about the property itself.
Purchaser	Buyer of a property.
Registered land	Land with title registered with H.M. Land Registry.
Restrictive covenants	Clauses forbidding certain activities and uses of the property and land.
Stamp duty	Tax on some legal documents including deeds and documents relating to sale of property.
Title deeds	Documents showing true ownership of a property.
Transfer	Document transferring ownership of a property with registered title to the new owner.
Vacant possession	A property left completely empty by seller for purchaser to move into.
Vendor	Seller of a property.

Index